THE SHADOW ON MY SHOULDER

TREVOR VERNER

A catalogue record for this
work is available from the
National Library of Australia

National Library of Australia Catalogue-in-Publication data:
The Shadow on my Sholder/Trevor Verner

ISBN: 978-0-6452641-7-3 (Paperback)
ISBN: 978-0-6452641-8-0 (Ebook)

To the memory of Ronnie Verner

Men's Mental Health
by Dr Tim Bingham MRCGP

Worrying trend as data shows male suicide rate highest in twenty years

Suicide is a major health problem, and the global suicide mortality rate amounts to 1.4% of all deaths worldwide. Most suicides are related to psychiatric disease, with depression, substance use disorders and psychosis being the most relevant risk factors. However, anxiety, personality, eating and trauma-related disorders, as well as organic mental disorders, also contribute.

Suicide prevention efforts often depend on the disclosure of suicidal ideation (thoughts or plans to self-harm) which is an early step in the suicidal process.

Depression is strongly related to both suicidal ideation and attempt, but it lacks specificity as a predictor. Depression and substance use disorders, mostly alcohol, are the most prevalent diagnoses among suicide victims.

The suicide rate in Northern Ireland is one of the highest in the world.

For 2017, Northern Ireland had the highest rate in the UK (and Ireland) of registered deaths by suicide for men (29.1 per 100,000 men) and women (8.5 per 100,000 women).

On 19 December 2018, *The Belfast Telegraph* reported that, "More men die by suicide in Northern Ireland than anywhere else in the UK." In the article, Samaritans Ireland director, Cindy O'Shea, added that the number of women taking their own lives in Northern Ireland has reduced, but that the total suicide rate has increased, due to a rise in male suicide.

Simon Gunning, CEO of Campaign Against Living Miserably (CALM), said, "Though society has become more caring around the mental health issue, more support is still needed to do whatever we can to stop its prevalence."

The potential impact of the coronavirus pandemic – Mr Gunning added that, "During the coronavirus crisis the charity's helpline had seen a 35-40% increase in the number of calls it was receiving. Across board have seen a heightening of national levels of anxiety. Clearly people are in need of help and this can't become a forgotten casualty."

Undoubtedly, the pandemic has affected everyone in society, but the Samaritans are particularly worried about three groups: people with pre-existing mental health conditions; young people who self-harm; and less well-off middle-aged men. They emphasise that it is essential that these groups are given the support they need before people reach crisis point.

Mental 'wellness' is something that is often overlooked when looking at health issues. Perhaps because mental illnesses are simply not as visual as physical illnesses; they are often harder to spot or diagnose.

The most important way we can promote mental wellness is by changing the public's understanding of mental illness. It must be recognised that mental illnesses are serious diseases that require medical intervention. It is essential people do not feel ashamed or embarrassed for seeking treatment of a psychological problem.

Cultural acknowledgement of mental illness is not something that will come about quickly. It will take time and effort from both the public and the medical community. The most important way cultural acknowledgement can be achieved is through education and raising awareness as in this book.

Some of the perceived problems of reaching men with the mental health education message are listed below.

1. Awareness strategies are not targeted well to men.

Men respond more strongly to humor – men 'check out' as soon as they see mention of mental health. This can cause men to feel out of place or vulnerable when discussing these issues.

2. Men ask for help differently.

Men are much more likely to accept help when there is a chance for reciprocity – that is, when they perceive an opportunity to help the other person in return. This wards off the feeling of 'weakness' that is often associated with asking for help. Men also prefer to either fix or at least try to fix issues when possible, before reaching out for help. It helps if they see it as another car part to replace or a wall to patch up – by approaching it this way, you may start to find meaningful ways to communicate.

3. Men can express mental health problems differently, leading to mis- or under-diagnosis.

Although men and women experience similar symptoms of some mental health concerns, how they manifest and present those symptoms can vary. For example, women often respond to symptoms of depression with a more recognisable affect – they might appear disheartened, sad, or express that they feel worthless. Although men can demonstrate this as well, they are also more likely to present a more irritable affect – anger, frustration, impulsivity, or a variety of other behaviours that aren't always considered in the context of depression, such as increased alcohol consumption. These are often seen as normal male behaviours and can therefore mask the signs of depression to themselves, friends and family and the less well-informed.

Consider whether these reasons apply to you and if you are looking after your mental health as well as your physical health.

Coping Tips
• Reach out – chat to a friend when you start to hide yourself away
• Be listened to – have a chat and get it off your chest with a friend or helpline
• Keep up with your routine – or add new structure to your day
• Get outside for a short walk
• Use a motivational playlist or motivational quote to inspire you to keep going
• Do something you're good at
• Do something new like volunteering
• Take up a new hobby
• Get out of your comfort zone – feel a sense of achievement from this
• Breathe in to a count of ten and out to a count of ten. Repeat ten times
• Switch off – in a way that works for you, with a book, film, video game etc.
• Do something with your hands like painting a wall or cooking to get out of your head

- Ask a friend how they are – doing something for a friend can make you feel better
- Eat well and drink in moderation
- Stop and pause – take time to check in with your head by using mindfulness, writing or meditation

Many of these coping strategies are incorporated in Trevor's pencil drawing classes which have been such a great help and support to his participants as they try to deal with their psychological distress. This book highlighting men's mental health issues is also clearly very timely as we try to transition out of the covid pandemic.

Need support?

If you are feeling like ending your life, please call 999 or go to A&E and ask for the contact of the nearest crisis resolution team. These are teams of mental health care professionals who work with people in severe distress.

- If you need someone to talk to then Samaritans are available on 116 123 (UK) for free, 24/7. They are there to talk to, listen and they won't judge or tell you what to do.
- C.A.L.M.: National helpline for men to talk about any troubles they are feeling. Call 0800 58 58 58 (UK). They are available 5pm-midnight 365 days a year.
- For support in a crisis, Text Shout to 85258. If you're experiencing a personal crisis, are unable to cope and need support. Shout can help with urgent issues such as: suicidal thoughts, abuse or assault, self-harm, bullying and relationship challenges.

Foreword
by Emma Weaver, Mental Wealth International

Mental health impacts each and every one of us. The WHO defines mental health as a state of wellbeing in which the individual realises their own abilities, can cope with the normal stresses of life, can work productively and fruitfully, and is able to make a contribution to society. Whilst this is a very broad definition it gives a foundation to understand a positive aspect of mental health.

I believe throughout different times of our lives we go from positive mental health to negative mental health periods. Things happen and we all experience life differently. I am not, however, speaking about those who are impacted by mental illness, trauma and/or other circumstances.

I have worked in mental health and wellbeing recovery services, day services, floating support, residential and supported housing, and came to realise a long time ago that one size does not fit all. Each person is different and a person-centred approach is paramount. I also understand that this is not always accessible to everyone and resources are unfortunately limited. This does not, however, mean all is lost. A new approach to supporting those who are experiencing mental health issues, may it be depression, trauma, addiction or PTSD, there are new and innovative approaches evolving and are as effective as many that came before.

I have worked within Inspire Wellbeing all throughout my career and have enjoyed the many services that I have been involved with and it is here that I had the pleasure of working with Trevor – the gentleman whom has been so brave to write this book which, I assure you, has been no easy task. Trevor visits two of our services every week facilitating a pencil art class. Now, whilst pencil art may seem a little random, I have come to see the benefits firsthand as our members continue to grow through their wellbeing journey. Art therapy can improve holistic health, strengthen focus, improve mood and much more. The participants of the groups that Trevor facilitates report to feel more productive and see improvement in their mood and a sense of achievement when complete. This I feel is an essential part of wellbeing – setting goals, intentions or tasks, whatever they may be, provides a much more favourable outcome than one may realise when attending the classes.

With suicide rates at a very high level and initiatives created to support those impacted by suicide and those who have contemplated it, creating a safe space to express yourself, talk if you want or not if you do not want, being part of a group or community, all acts as a huge support for people. I often feel that when you provide a space where there is an activity or a small distraction taking place, this allows people to open up and tap in to their feelings and a conversation can happen while one part of their brain is concentrating on the task in hand while the other is open to talk.

I often find the most open conversations that I have with

my children is in the car or walking side by side with no eye contact and a small distraction allowing them to be free with their words.

Lived experience is an essential part of supporting others on their wellbeing journey. It provides, hope, empathy, understanding and a non-judgemental environment for many to feel supported and find what works for them. Using a holistic approach gives options and provides a person-centred approach. Moving away from the one size fits all. We need to listen and learn from those who have experienced mental health difficulties or even live with a mental health issue on a daily basis and learn from their experiences and support people to speak out about it as it will heal so many and reduce the existing stigma surrounding mental health.

Through my role with Mental Wealth International, I encourage and support people to look after and maintain their mental health at all times and do not wait until they may feel unwell to start implementing strategies for positive mental health. It is what we do every day and our routines that form the basis for our wellbeing. Thriving with positive mental wealth instead of always striving for it can be achieved by mindfully looking after our mental health with meditation, yoga, walks, talking to a friend, joining a group or even a hobby. These can all add to maintaining and achieving optimum wellbeing.

It is so important to always reach out no matter how big or small you feel the issue is. This book will provide a platform to start many conversations and help so many. After all, it is good to talk.

The picture reminds me of the forge in Lisbellaw, where I grew up.
I loved the smell of the forge.

Chapter One

There are nine children in my family, then Mum and Dad. So I have a family of eleven; six boys and three girls including my twin sister. We were the youngest for seven years until my little brother came along. As a child I was always drawing or doing scribbles on pieces of paper. I also loved listening to music, so any chance I got I would sit at the kitchen table with head-phones on and draw. My mum was always very encouraging about the drawing, I think because one of her brothers enjoyed sketching – she always talked about his drawing. My primary school teacher always got me to draw things up on the black-board in class with chalk. If there were any posters to make, I was given the task to do them. It was great at the time because it made me feel important. I was never an academic pupil, I just enjoyed doing things with my hands like woodwork and metal-work. Cathy Cook was my art teacher in secondary school, and it was her who encouraged me to do my art because she felt I had a great talent in pencil drawing.

We were a very close family. As a boy growing up, I had a lovely childhood surrounded by my big brothers and sisters, and we had some special times as a family. Christmas, for me, was a really exciting time, there was always a great buzz in the build-up to the festive season. Mum was hard at work preparing for the celebrations. I loved the smell of home cooking, especially the smell of Christmas puddings and cake. The smell of baked cakes was in the air for weeks. School still played a part; we were making Christmas decorations for the assembly hall because they were giving the school a festive look.

My story really begins at Christmas, 1975. I was twelve years of age, a young boy wondering what life had in store for me, what adventures I would have. Little did I know that it was going to be the start of something traumatic and frightening – a dark time in my life.

Chapter Two

Christmas holidays from school had arrived. I was outside playing with my close friends who lived in my park. We were talking about Christmas and what we might get from the big guy with the white beard. I knew that my brothers and sisters would be at home for Christmas as well. It was going to be an exciting time with my family. Christmas Eve had arrived, the atmosphere was amazing. We were all in such good form, the house was full of Christmas cheer – the colourful lights on the tree gave out such a warm glow.

It was time for me to go to bed, but later that night my eldest brother, Ronnie, came up the stairs. He was in the bathroom when he called me and asked me to help him fasten a chain around his neck. As I put it on I asked him what it was. He said that it was a St Christopher that his girlfriend had got him and it was to keep him safe when travelling.

He then said, 'Ted,' (that was a wee name he called me) 'you get back into bed, Santa's coming tonight.' He also said, 'I'll see you on Boxing Day.' He was going to work on night duty and also working on Christmas morning so that he could be off later. He was going to his girlfriend's house for Christmas afternoon. Ronnie was such a nice person. I used to wash his car and do wee chores for him when I could. He would often get me to blow-dry his hair – we just had a very relaxed brotherly relationship. Sleeping that night was so hard because I was thinking about Christmas morning. About six in the morning my sister and I woke and were so excited to see what Santa had left under the tree. We got our presents and Mum got up early to get the turkey on. With a big family to feed, she spent the whole morning doing jobs to make our Christmas dinner special. We played with our toys and also helped out with things getting ready for the big day that was ahead. The smells in the house were amazing, everybody was in good form, Christmas music playing in the background, it was just lovely. Little did we know what trauma and devastation would be inflicted on us as a family later on that day.

Dad was working so he was due home at 4 o'clock. The day was a real winter's day – it was raining, the fire was on, it was burning with hot coals making us feel snug and warm. My face was glowing, and we were all huddled around watching television. There was so much on that day. The highlight of the programs for me was the film *The Wizard of Oz*. I can remember so clearly. We were all sitting down on the floor, Dad had come home and he was resting comfortably in the chair. The lights in the house were down low, Mum had opened a box of sweets, the film had started, and we were well into the film when a knock came on the door. I remember Dad getting up and going into the hall. He closed the door and went to see who was there. We were still watching the film. He came into the room, put the light on straight away and said, 'Ronnie has been in an accident, it's not good, bad accident.'

For me, as a twelve-year-old boy, it felt that time had stopped, there and then.

Seeing all my brothers and sisters crying and Mum so distressed, I wanted to help but couldn't. I felt so helpless even at that age – my mind was in freefall; I didn't know how to react. One minute I was crying, the next I was staring silently wondering if Ronnie would be okay. I wasn't to know that this was really the start of my mental health being affected by a trauma.

Mum and Dad and the older members of the family went into the hospital to see Ronnie. I didn't go because I was scared, so my twin sister and I stayed with my next-door neighbour. It was a long evening; my mind was all over the place wondering what was going to happen. Later that night, the family came home. Ronnie had died in the early hours of Boxing Day. When coming home from work he had crashed his car and suffered a severe head injury, due to being thrown out of the back window. Dad had to make the decision to have the life support machine switched off as Ronnie would never have made a full recovery. That must have been the most heart-wrenching thing for any mother or father to have to do for their child, no matter what age. Ronnie was only twenty-one.

There was, I felt, a real dark shadow that had fallen on the family. Everyone was so sad, people were crying. Mum kept a wee fire on that night. I remember hearing sobbing and yet times of quietness, obviously brothers and sisters deep in thought about Ronnie. Some of them went to bed but I know I got no sleep thinking about him. That next day was so hard, I had never seen my dad so upset. He had been so brave for everyone on Christmas Day, but he just broke down when we were all back home. It was so hard to listen to family members talking about Ronnie's funeral. This was so final – we were never going to see him again.

During that time I can remember people visiting us in the house. People just kept coming and talking to Mum and Dad and the rest of the family. I didn't get to go to his funeral because the youngest of us were kept away and were sent round to another neighbour's house. We were told it was a very big funeral, and people continued to call for days afterwards.

Christmas was never the same again.

There was just this void. I missed Ronnie's big smile, his great sense of humour. He was my hero. He was so fit having been involved in so many sports – swimming, badminton, football and athletics were his favourites. It was just so hard to accept, even at twelve years of age, that Ronnie was gone.

Chapter Three

School holidays were over, and people were trying to get back to normal – whatever normal could be. When I went to school, teachers were saying how sorry they were about Ronnie. He was well-liked, and our family were well-known.

School was hard for me because I couldn't concentrate in class. My art was the only subject that I could lose myself in. I could let all the pain and sorrow out of my head. But when I came home, I could see and feel the sadness in the family. I tried to help Mum when I could, but she was so heartbroken. I was still so confused about it all. I knew Ronnie was gone but I couldn't express my feelings. I tried to ask questions about Ronnie but Mum found it hard to talk about it and I just felt so helpless.

In that first year after his death, there was so many strange thoughts and ideas going through my mind, obviously in relation to Ronnie's death. I missed him so much. I worried about what it must have been like for him, it must have been so scary as he lay on the ground injured, was there no-one around to help him? It must have been so lonely on that road, this all happened yet he was only a few miles from home. All these thoughts were going through my mind all the time.

Mum tried to tell me about Ronnie because I found it hard to see his face in my mind. I often went upstairs to the boys' bedroom – in the cupboard mum had a few bits of Ronnie's clothes. I got comfort from smelling them to get his scent. She gave me a small photo of him, he was just as I remembered.

Some time later I was outside playing with one my friends, it was raining so we went inside a wee tin shed that Dad had built at the back of the house. Mum kept bits and pieces in there and I noticed this plastic bag in the corner stuffed away. Being an inquisitive young boy, I decided to look closely at it, but I got such a shock! It was Ronnie's clothes from the accident. Obviously the police had given this bag to my mum and dad to bring home, and this is where they stored it at the time. I was so sad seeing this that I told my friend to go home. Then I nervously returned to the shed. I could see his shirt and trousers, the shirt was so red with blood, it was like living Christmas Day all over again. I cried and cried and I was so sad.

I did not say anything to Mum because I knew she could not deal with it. I knew that must be why it was still in the shed.

It was about late January and I was at home after school sitting in front of the fire warming myself. I will never forget what happened next – Mum had a good coal fire on, the embers were really red, she suddenly came in, never said anything to me, but what did she have in her hand? The plastic bag from the shed! She stuffed it in the fire and walked out of the room. I could hear her crying in the kitchen. I watched the clothes burn. I stared at that fire until every bit had gone. It is a strange thing to say but I felt it was another piece of Ronnie gone.

Chapter Four

A few months had passed and the mood was still sad. I felt that everyone had to deal with their own sadness. It annoyed me so much that I hadn't been at the funeral or to see him at the hospital. One day I said to Mum I was going down the town to get sweets. I walked down to our local churchyard where Ronnie was buried. When I got to the gates I was scared to go in, but I did. There was no-one about. To me it was so frightening to think that he was in the ground in that grave – but I still felt that I could talk to him.

So, I got down on my hunkers and I started to talk to Ronnie. I told him I missed him so much and that I wished I could have helped him. I never got to see him play badminton. I really was upset – I didn't care if anyone came into the graveyard. I just felt I was with my big brother again. I even suggested that I could dig him out with my bare hands. I said a wee prayer and left feeling that this is where I can keep in contact with him. I have often wondered since, how something like this could take such a chunk out of your life, and the mental pressure it caused me as a young boy.

This picture reminds me of my love for cowboy films.

Chapter Five

When I was in high school, Enniskillen High School as it was then, I was bullied for the first couple of years. Looking back, I know I lacked confidence in myself even then, and of course this was picked up in the classroom by the bullies. It wasn't until later on that I confronted them. It was then I noticed, when I stood up for myself, they didn't bother me again. This I feel was all due to grief affecting my mental health.

I never reported the bullying to the teachers, but I did get comfort from them in other ways. They knew Ronnie and the rest of the children as we all attended the same school. For many years I felt the death of Ronnie had left a scar that I carried all the time. I frequently had sad moments, I would find myself drifting away with my thoughts about Ronnie. I found that I got so much comfort working in my art classes and my metalwork and woodwork classes. It was these subjects that got me through my school years. Because I was working with my hands, my mind could relax. Sport was a big help also. All my brothers and sisters played a lot of sport. I was really drawn to badminton, just like the rest of the family. So after school, when I turned eighteen, I started playing. It was a sport that made me feel close to Ronnie even though I never saw him play. Everyone

I met through badminton knew him and my older brother John – they played together as men's doubles partners. I was so proud of the chats other people had with me about the boys playing in tournaments together. I feel that at this age mentally, I was getting a real fix from the stories, and as a player, I suppose, I wanted to be like Ronnie. When I left school I worked in a garden nursery for about two years. Even then, working with plants seemed to give that mental stimulation that I needed, even though I didn't realise at the time that I needed it. I joined the part-time reserve Police Force; my dad was a policeman and Ronnie was also a young serving constable when he died. I was drawn to this kind of career; I didn't know if it was the right thing for me or not but I progressed on for a few more years from part-time to full-time reserve.

It was when I hit the age of twenty-one and the realisation of just how young Ronnie really was when he died – and that he still had his whole life to live, that the pressure of things really affected me. It was like his death starting again. I missed him so much and I was having many sad times wondering what he would be doing now if he was alive. I began to understand how all the family must have felt and the trauma all of us had suffered. As I got older, I could understand the loss better.

Chapter Six

I was in the police for ten years. It was a tough job because of all the risks that were involved during 'The Troubles'. I served in many dangerous police stations during that time. I lost some colleagues to terrorism and had some near misses. At this time, I was still using my art and sport as a way to relax, I didn't understand then that I was struggling with my mental health – but I knew I felt better when I got the time to draw. Art was my help. While you knew the risks, you just went on, knowing what could happen to you, it was very stressful.

One morning when I was due to go up the town on the beat from the police station I was serving at in Enniskillen, we were attacked by terrorists. The station was hit with homemade mortars. Eighteen were fired, and nine hit the station. A mortar landed on top of the police car I was about to get into with two other colleagues, just outside the main door of the station. I had just got to the door ready to go out when, BANG! the car I was going to get into was blown up. All I can remember is lying on the floor wondering what had happened. We could hear all the other bombs going off, the station shaking with each explosion. When all went quiet, I went into real panic. I ran outside to try to get away from the building but there

was pandemonium – smoke and dust in the air, burning cars, people running everywhere – it was just confusion. Everyone seemed to be moving out of the police station to the public road. I wasn't 'injured'.

Someone ordered me to go up with a few others to direct traffic at the top of the street. When I got up there, my mind was so confused, my heart was thumping, the adrenaline was going through me at some rate. One minute I was directing traffic, then suddenly my mind and vision just went into slow motion. I was like a zombie in the middle of the road. I just stopped functioning. Someone realised I was in shock and sent me back to the station. It was only then when things became silent that I spoke to my authorities about where I was and how close I was to serious injury or death, that I was told to go home. I couldn't drive home as my car was damaged and because I was in so much shock so I was driven home. I remember speaking to Mum and Dad, he was due to start work that morning.

Mum made me a cup of tea, my head felt so heavy and my stomach felt sick so I went for a lie down. Every time I closed my eyes I kept reliving the same thing, so I just lay there, I had no control of the way my brain and body felt, obviously it was stress and shock. The thought that never left me was how lucky I was not to have been killed or seriously injured in this dreadful event. That afternoon it was on the news that no-one was killed but there were a lot of people like myself, who went through what I was going through. That night I couldn't sleep and when I did doze with fatigue, I woke up from a bang. I went to the doctor the next morning and he examined me and said that I was suffering from shock, trauma and stress from the incident so he put me on sick leave. He said for me to take a few weeks

off and see how I get on. This incident was a catalyst for my mental health.

Up to the time of the attack I was in the police reserve, but I was due to do the training for the regular police. But due to the attack I was put on sick leave. The blast had left me very confused; I was having nightmares and feeling fatigued. It was, for me, the downward slope of mental illness, I felt this shadow on my shoulder all the time. I had always wanted to be in the regular police but being confused and not knowing what the best decision was to make – it was like flipping a coin, when it lands, heads I go and tails I don't. Having suffered such a recent trauma and having no advice, I knew I had to make the decision myself, even though I was in a vulnerable state. I didn't want to miss my chance when the training depot was still in Enniskillen. I had the exams passed, ready for the date of entry to training. That was just before the incident happened. There was this pull on me, and so I made the decision to go, really not in control of my feelings.

I made the call-up date and went in to training; twenty-one weeks in Enniskillen and seven weeks in Belfast. Within a few weeks, I knew I had made the wrong decision, but I felt trapped because I thought that if I gave up and left, people would think I was a failure. So rather than see if that came true, I had to grin and bear it and carry on. That was the way I felt.

I found it hard to finish the training no matter how hard I tried. Believe it or not, I felt lonely and scared even though there were plenty of people to chat to. When I was doing things, I smiled and pretended to be happy. But when we finished for the day, there was just me and my thoughts during the night. When the weeks passed a lot of the squad were really excited about finishing. I couldn't share that excitement – I just wanted to see the end.

When the passing out parade came round, I was allocated my station. I was scared, worried and wondering what was ahead of me. I knew I was still suffering mentally from the effects of the trauma, as my sleeping was affected and the night terrors were still happening. But I was still carrying on as if nothing was wrong, always in this battle with an invisible enemy. I didn't go home at weekends because I felt slightly ashamed of myself, as if I was still letting people down. For two years this was eating away at me like a silent disease. I was getting so confused with life; I didn't want to talk to people the same as before, I was waking up crying in the mornings, I started to let my health go, I lost interest in how I looked, I stopped shaving. My mind would wander into this blankness, I felt I was of no importance.

One day when I was out in the car, I was thinking that if I was killed that day it would be for the best, no-one would miss me. I remember being in Castlewellan Police Station, where myself and two other guys lived. I was making tea when another colleague came up behind me and hit a steel canopy with a stick. He only did it for a joke, but it scared me so much. I relived the bangs from the blasts in Enniskillen and I ran out of the station to the perimeter fence thinking that we were under attack. That's how fragile I was getting due to mental stress. It was at this point I knew I really needed to say something. I felt like I was a snowman just slowly melting away till there was nothing left.

Chapter Seven

When I came in from work in my rest times I went to my room in the station. I had done some drawings and they were on the wall. I got comfort from looking at them and they calmed me.

This particular day, I knew it was time to talk. My sergeant was a nice wee man, I walked down to his office and went in to see him and said, 'Could we have a chat for a minute?'

I started to tell him how I was feeling. I felt as if I was in freefall and going out of control with my life. I just broke down, I cried and sobbed but within ten minutes he had reassured me that he could help and get me support. After a good chat he said I should go on the sick and stay on it till I was sorted.

My first port of call was the police medical officer. I went to see him and we had a very deep conversation about the past year and the way I was feeling. I knew there was something going on in my head, but it was so mixed up. I knew I had been hurting for so long, I was emotionally exhausted. When he finished talking to me, he said that I would need to be seen for further help by a psychiatrist and a psychologist. It was after him saying this that he said, 'Trevor, we are going to take your gun from you, as a precaution, because of what you have told me.' It was about a month before I got to see the psychiatrist and psychologist.

I felt I was freefalling from then. I tried to do things to keep my mind busy – I loved playing badminton, so I kept that up and tried to focus on doing some drawing. Even though I was doing things, in my head it felt like there was another person in there, talking and pulling at me. I was exhausted fighting this battle. While this was going on, I had to go into hospital to get keyhole surgery on my knee. This was yet another thing on my mind, but I was in and out on the one day and the surgery was a success. I was staying in a room at Bangor Police Station at this time, only going home on an odd occasion.

This month felt like an eternity, and I knew I was getting worse. I wasn't sleeping well and when I did, I would wake up in the morning crying. I couldn't be bothered washing or shaving. For days I just stayed in my room with the curtains pulled. I felt so lonely and as if I was trapped. Everything was going through my mind, just a constant roller-coaster of thoughts.

One evening I went to visit my brother, Davy, and his wife. I put a brave face on and enjoyed my chat but deep down I wanted to really talk to them about how I felt, but something was stopping me, fear and embarrassment probably. After saying goodbye I left and went back to Bangor, I remember driving, crying, my mind was so confused, I was seeing things outside but could hear no sound, it was like being in a silent movie.

I went back to my room and got the drugs I had been pre-scribed for the pain in my knee.

I was feeling so sad thinking about my past – Ronnie, Mum, Dad, my brothers and sisters.

I drove to a shop, got a can of coke and went and parked in

a car park. I was crying, I felt worthless and had a feeling of letting everyone I know down.

At this stage I wanted to end it all – it was the only way I could see to stop the pain.

I remember writing a note about missing Ronnie, and to say sorry to my brothers and sisters.

I wrote a note to Mum and Dad saying that I was sorry but I couldn't cope anymore, and that no-one could understand how I felt. It was then that I took the tablets – about fifteen strong pain killers.

I was sitting for about forty-five minutes crying.

Then something came over me. I phoned my brother and asked him to ask his wife, Inez, who was a nurse, if the pain killers were strong. Then I made my excuses and finished the phone call. I then drove straight to a local pub that I went to every now and again in Bangor.

I sat at the bar and had a few vodkas. My head was in this haze. I was there for a while just staring at the wall when suddenly I heard a voice saying my name. It was my brother, Davy. He asked if I was okay and I just broke down and said I was so sorry and told him I had taken an overdose with the tablets and then had alcohol on top.

Davy made me go into the toilet and make myself sick. When we went outside and got into his car, I had to be taken to the hospital to be checked out.

When we got to the hospital I was put into a waiting room to see the doctor. All I could say at that moment was that I was sorry, and that I didn't mean to do it. When the doctor arrived he asked me questions about how I was feeling, what I had taken, how many tablets, how much I'd had to drink. Again, all

I could say to him was that I was sorry and that I didn't mean to do it. The doctor said making myself sick was the best thing I could have done but that he couldn't know how much of the tablets my body had absorbed. He gave me a tablet to line my stomach and said to Davy that I would need to go home with someone and for them to keep a watch on me, but if nothing happens I should be okay from the overdose.

I did recover physically over the next couple of days, but I was so disappointed in myself for what I did. I knew I was still depressed and anxious, nothing had changed with my mental health, if anything it left me filled with remorse, feeling that I was selfish and guilty for upsetting my family by doing what I had just done. The doctor was convinced, that in his opinion, I had difficulties and this was a cry for help.

Later on that month I got the go-ahead to see the psychiatrist and psychologist. I saw them for three months. It was like having your mind stripped back to the start of life. It was so moving and sad and full of crying. They asked me in detail about myself and my family life. They encouraged me to talk in detail about the trauma of losing Ronnie, about the funeral, the grieving process, things I was doing, work, hobbies, sport – every aspect of my life. They covered everything right up to the breakdown and suicide attempt.

Each time I went I listened and cried a lot. I found that breaking all the parts down and talking – this word TALKING – was and is, key. I was feeling better as each session went on. They helped me to see the reasons for certain things in my life. They talked about dealing with worries and stress, teaching me to deal with them and getting them out of my head. My brain was overloaded so I was advised to try not to worry about the small things. The first thing they wanted me to do was to be positive. They encouraged me to keep up my sport, to use my talent as an artist, to keep doing my drawing because it was very therapeutic for me, to see friends and not to be scared to go out. They said to keep talking and one very important thing, to not ever be afraid to talk to someone if I was worried, no matter how silly it might seem. They were very keen to help me get through this by using my own skills, which would help my confidence, and to do it without medication.

My diagnosis was that I had a mental breakdown caused mainly by the death of Ronnie, a family member, at a young age, seeing the upset and hurt on other family members, particularly the trauma on my mother and father. Growing up with that hurt, missing him as I got older, was hard to deal with. Then going into a dangerous job like the police force, seeing things to do with death, accidents, and the loss of colleagues, all added to the stress. They said that having been involved in the mortar attack on the police station definitely contributed to the mental breakdown and that I was suffering from post-traumatic stress disorder. Also, they felt that this being one of the recent traumas I should seriously consider leaving the police to really get away from the memories and stress related to that job.

While I was undergoing my therapy, I stayed either at the station or with my twin sister Sandra, and her husband Richard. I owe them a lot for understanding me and for listening to my worries. They took me out and about and I still met people, they were a big help and support to me until I could make my decisions clearly, I thank them from my heart.

I was still on sick leave so I made an appointment with the force medical officer. He was kind and understanding, he had seen my medical report and we chatted over the findings and about how I was feeling. He said, 'Trevor, I could send you to another area to work but I feel the problems would still be there. I agree the best thing is to start fresh and get away from the police.'

After a few days thinking what to do, I made the decision to end all this stress and resign.

It was a Monday and I was still living between police stations and my sister's. I came downstairs in the station and went into my sergeant's office. I thanked him for helping me before and told him that I was just letting him know that I was heading down home. I told him I was resigning from the police and he asked me if I was sure. I just replied, 'I am so certain on this one.' I thanked him again.

He shook my hand and said, 'I wish you all the best in whatever you do next in life.'

When I was driving down that road home, I knew I would always have post-traumatic stress, but I knew from what I talked about with the psychiatrist and psychologist that I could hold my head high and I could do a lot to help myself.

It was about ten o'clock when I got home to Fermanagh, my dad was a traffic policeman for many years, and at that time was in charge of the traffic wardens in Enniskillen, so his office was in the police station.

When I went in, he was surprised to see me. He said, 'What are you at, are you still on the sick?'

I just said, 'Dad, yes I am, but I am making a decision today that hopefully will change my life. Can I use your typewriter?'

He said, 'What do you need that for?'

I just looked at him and said, 'I am starting a new life for myself, I just want peace from the pressure I've been under, I am typing out my resignation and then I'm walking over to the main station and handing it in.'

There was just silence from Dad, but as I was leaving he said, 'If you have given it thought then you know what you are doing, Trevor.'

I went into the station and put the letter in the post for headquarters.

As soon as I handed it in and walked out that door, the weight just lifted off me, I felt like a free man. About two weeks later I was contacted to hand in all of my police equipment and that was the end of that.

Chapter Eight

My new life was something I was excited about. I didn't know what I was going to do but I knew I still had to work in order to live and to keep my mental health good. I was lucky to be given that second chance and I owe that to my brother Davey and his wife Inez, I will always be grateful to them both. I felt I had the tools now to help me continue in life.

When I was growing up my family always talked about one of them going to New Zealand because my Dad's brother and family lived there. I remember Uncle Jack and his lovely wife Olga came to visit Mum and Dad. They had four of a family, Grant, Jeanette, Anne and Michael. Anne and Jeanette had come over a few years after their parents, so we all felt a connection to them and when I was deciding what to do, New Zealand came into my mind as an option. I felt that this was the best place to get away to recuperate for a while – it felt safe to go and stay with family, so I decided to contact Uncle Jack to see what he thought.

I think that I was the last person my parents thought would go, so they were shocked when I announced that I had bought my ticket. I planned to go and have a holiday first and then look for work, and just see how things would work out. So one day I went into town and bought a return ticket as a security, so that if things didn't work out I could come home again.

Mum and Dad were at tea one day day when I said, 'I have something to tell you both. I have written to Uncle jack and have my ticket bought. I leave in December for New Zealand.' They didn't believe me until I showed them the ticket.

I sold my car and got things sorted and I even had a wee going away party. It was lovely to have all the family and my close friends there for the night because I was hoping that I might stay in New Zealand if the opportunity arose. I was hoping it would be the best break to help me relax and help my mental health at the same time. I had something to focus on, and this was going to be the first part of my jigsaw of my new life. For someone who had only ever been away once on a holiday to Spain, this was a big move on my own.

When the time came to leave, Dad drove me up to the airport. In my mind I was excited but sad to be leaving home, because there was a chance that I might not be back. I flew through London, Bangkok, Singapore, Melbourne, Sydney, Auckland and finally landed in Wellington and I really enjoyed the journey. It was exciting and I got the opportunity to talk to lots of people. We had a long delay in London due to fog, so the passengers were all put up in a hotel for three nights. Most people seemed unfazed by the delay and were in a partying mood, so we got the chance to bond and have some fun. I was feeling great. Having been through such a bad year, it was amazing to me to be able to have the confidence for the first time to be flying so far away on my own. It felt so good.

It took about twenty-four hours to get there. When the plane was landing in Wellington, I had butterflies in my tummy. I was nervous but also excited. I could hardly believe that I was there – I had already achieved something big for me. I finally got through immigration and out to the car park where Uncle Jack and Olga were waiting for me. We hugged and I remember him saying that he was so proud to have one of George's (my dad) sons there, we were all very emotional. It was hard to believe I was so far away from home.

I had a lovely time with my uncle and his family; they were so kind to me when I was there. I needed this time away from Northern Ireland to think about my life.

The time then came when I needed to apply for jobs. My uncle and I talked about me living with them until I got work – he would keep me as a resident there until I got my citizenship. This was a great opportunity for me, but two months had passed and I had struggled to find even part-time work. It was bad timing because students were just out of college, and New Zealand's laws at the time favoured their own citizens over immigrants. I just couldn't get a job. I was put into a position where I felt I couldn't stay with my uncle for anything long-term and my money would run out waiting for jobs that might not happen. I had a chat to him and said I would be heading home after three months if I didn't get work. He was disappointed but he understood. It was a shame because I enjoyed my time there and New Zealand is a beautiful country.

When the time came to go home, Uncle Jack and Auntie Olga took me to the airport. It was very emotional for us all. My uncle had tears in his eyes as he told me I was welcome back any time. This part in my life was meant to be. Although my adventure to New Zealand didn't result in finding a job and staying there, I still felt very proud of myself for having the confidence to go and for being the first and only one of my family to make that trip. I had been through so much, having a complete break and spending time with my Uncle and Aunt and their family helped in my recovery.

Chapter Nine

I knew when I got back home to Northern Ireland I was ready to carry on, but I still knew that I would always have to be careful with my mental health. New Zealand played a big part in helping me. I know that some doors open and some close, but there's always a reason, and I believe this was meant to have happened.

Sadly, Uncle Jack passed away a few years later from a heart attack, but I have great memories of him and the help and support that he and Olga gave me. He was a lovely man and I will always remember him fondly.

My trip home was unusual in that our flight took a detour through Russian airspace due to Russia having opened their airspace for a short time, we were escorted for part of the journey by two MIG fighter jets fully laden with missiles and flying so close to us that we could actually see the pilot. When we were leaving the Russian airspace the two planes backed off and the pilot on our side actually gave us a thumbs up, it was quite an experience.

Being back home was another challenge, I was working out my options to see how I would get settled back in my home-town. My first big test was finding a place to live and getting a job. I had left a job where I was earning a great salary, so being on an income support of £37 a week was a big shock, and I worried about how I would manage. I had to make a fresh start and that was more important to me than the money. The most important thing for me was to keep positive and remember things would get better.

I got my first job in a filling station helping out and serving petrol, it was a starting point. I was staying with my sister at the time, and she and her husband were very understanding to my situation. I could talk to them about past things as well as my worries and appreciated the company. The wee job was very different to my role in the police. It helped me have a different outlook on my life working as a civilian – it didn't have the same restrictions and pressures of life as in the police force at that time. I still had my interest in art and sports, and I had a few good friends that I could pick up with again. I was still recovering from the mental health issues, and this was something that I would have to continually work at, and again these were the things that would help me get my life back together again. My sister Sandra and her husband were instrumental in getting me started and getting my mind into that normal everyday pattern. I stayed with them for about a year or so. I knew that the mental health issue was going to be slow. I didn't know if the time scale would be months, years, or if I would always have this illness. I was just going to embrace life and be thankful to be given a second chance with the people around me, my friends and especially my family.

The next opportunity I got was going to work for a kitchen manufacturer. Taking this job was good for me because it suited my frame of mind. I was working with my hands and I got a bit of a chance to use my creative side to some extent. With the job, I got the opportunity to move into a flat in the town centre. Moving into my own flat was just so exciting. I really appreciated what Sandra had done for me and I would never forget it, but this was a chance for me to stand on my own two feet and embrace the next chapter. I liked living in the flat because I could walk to work, and it was central for meeting friends. I also had the space there to draw. My drawing was key to my mental health because I found it so stimulating. I had read in a book that pencil drawing was more stimulating than colour because the concentration was more intense when just using black and white.

I continued to work there for about a year.

Two years had passed now, and my life was getting back on track but it was still a slow process. I was feeling better, I had a completely different view of life and I was more relaxed as a person. I actually became a better listener. These were indicators that the decisions I had made were right for me. Things were so much better – I wasn't letting things get on top of me, I was following the advice that the professionals had given me, and as time went by, I gained more confidence and began to enjoy life again. I moved to another job as a store hand in a firm working with car parts. I was involved in stocking, deliveries, loading and unloading trucks. I enjoyed that job because I liked the type of work and there was good camaraderie among the people who worked there. Also, the work wasn't too taxing. I felt that jobs in general had to have a lot of elements that helped me as a person with a mental health issue. I knew I had to respect this issue because I felt that if I was to rush things and not be careful then what I had struggled to build up could unravel and

I couldn't risk that. So for that reason I wasn't going to work at something that I felt was going to make me unhappy again. Outside of work I kept myself active playing my sport, doing my art and seeing my friends.

I also moved to a new flat while I was working there. I never wanted to share a flat with anyone because I felt by being on my own, I could fight the mental health head-on and in my own time. I knew that it could have been the wrong thing for me to do, because isolation is not good for your mental health, but I needed that time alone to work things out for myself and I felt I did the right thing for me. I still had the nightmares due to the post-traumatic stress, that was an ongoing battle, but I felt that if I could get the balance right in my waking life then I could have a normal life and be as much in control as possible.

Chapter Ten

While I was settling into my new job and flat, I found a direction in my life that I always wanted but never thought I could achieve. I was on a night out with my friends when I met a lovely girl. I knew when I saw her that she was 'the one'. Her name is Gloria and we have been together ever since. Gloria is a few years older than me, but I never thought that was a problem. She has a lovely personality – she's very calming and a great person to talk to. She seemed so solid and grounded and had different life experiences to me, but had also suffered the early loss of her father and a broken marriage.

Having had a feeling of no self-worth for years, and then trying to build myself up – mind, body and soul – to where I was, I knew I could bring a lot of myself to this relationship with love, kindness and honesty. I knew that I was still going to have to protect my mental health, but I had confidence in myself to control things and work at it, and try not to let it damage my new life. Being with Gloria was a turning point for me, she helped me a lot and I gained in confidence and started to believe in myself.

When Gloria and I met she already had two small boys, Ross and Peter, four and two. Having a lot of older brothers and sisters who were already married, I had quite a few nieces and nephews, so I was used to young children and liked being around them. So when I met the boys I was able to embrace the whole situation and enjoyed being a part of the family. Gloria's help, support, kindness, love and commitment helped me not to feel vulnerable, but very special. I got to love Gloria and the boys, this gave me the drive to try and better myself. This was such a turnaround from having no self-worth. I moved in with Gloria after about a year and we became a family.

Soon after I moved in, I lost my job and had to change direction yet again. Gloria and I got talking about the things that inspired me, and we tried to make a link between the kind of things I could do for work and the things I enjoyed doing. We came up with a few ideas. I knew art and sport were going to be there, because I was still doing the things I had to do to protect my mental health. Whatever I decided to look at, it needed to be something that I liked doing, that I could be in control of, and that would be stimulating for my mental health. Gloria encouraged me to consider self-employment so that I could have a day job at something active, and then keep my art as a way to relax in the evenings and work towards an exhibition.

We decided on me taking the plunge to become a self-employed painter and decorator, as I had learned something about the trade when I was younger in a part-time job. This was such a big decision for me because it was something hopefully that I could do for many years and keep my art running alongside. I looked into the process of getting started, and got help from a business startup scheme. I couldn't have imagined a few years earlier that I would be starting my own business, and have the confidence to make a new life for myself. I am very proud of myself. I think it's important to give yourself a clap on the back when you know you deserve it.

I was always told when I was in recovery that I shouldn't be afraid to talk, which has given me the confidence to talk to anyone about anything. It certainly helped me to go out and speak about my new venture and sell myself. Gloria's support and help was always there – it was so good to know that someone always had my back.

Time moved on happily and we were still dealing with things as a couple, talking and sharing things together. I felt we had a good tight family unit. It was then we had our third child, Daniel. We were so pleased he was brought into the world a healthy wee boy. My business was busy, my art was still going and I was considering an art exhibition. This would be the first time to show my work. I had been working so much with art for my stimulation that I felt the time was right. This was also a turning point because I felt it would be a proper start of my art professionally, to have people view it and give me feedback.

I always found that being an artist makes you look more at the creative side of things, and even when you see things around you in colour, you can imagine what they would look like in black and white. I do feel sometimes that a colour picture taken, then made into black and white, looks better to the eye. Also, I find it a lot harder to draw from the colour images and put them into pencil work with all the shades.

The opening night of the exhibition arrived and I remember that about eighty people turned up for the opening. Wine and cheese was served and there was a real celebratory feeling in the room. All the years of working and bringing my drawings up to a level that is accepted professionally, was so worth it. What a feeling just standing in the room knowing that all these people were there to see my work. Hours of drawing leading to this night. I was so proud of myself and I was so proud that I used the art for my recovery, and now I was taking my art onto the next level.

I remember walking round the room talking to people, listening to what they were saying about my style and work. It was important for me to understand that everyone who was in the room was there to support me and enjoy the exhibition, but I knew that I had to accept the fact that some people might not like the pencil art. The choice of art for your home is a very personal thing that all artists have to respect.

To be able to get everyone's attention in the room and being able to talk to them about my work and thanking them for coming was a beautiful feeling and one that increased my strength as an artist. Listening to what everyone has to say just makes you a better artist because you take it onboard. I love what I do when drawing but it's nice also to sell your work, and over the years, I have been able to sell my work locally, throughout Ireland and USA.

I was very proud to have my mum and dad at the exhibition. I do feel that Mum's encouragement to me as a young boy played a big part in my art and I am so grateful for that, I will never forget it.

The Dark Place

I went to bed in the dark feeling so alone
I woke in the mornings,
not by an alarm clock
But by a crying sound
Yes it was from me
Wakening up to your own cry, wondering what's wrong
Fuzzy head, confusion, actually being scared of your own self
Lying in the bed trying to put the pieces together of what has
been happening during the night
But yet all I got was blankness
When I calmed myself I moved to get up
Open the curtains, looking out of the window
All that I could think was, how am I going to get the day in
Never looking at the nice things the day has to offer, birds
singing, sun shining, thankful to be here.
I never got my clothes on with purpose
To do something good and exciting
I just had this cloud
Misty vision
Low self-esteem
The light was very far away down this long, long tunnel
I never felt I could get to that light no matter how it shone
bright.

The Light at the end of the Tunnel

When help comes your way you're so excited like a child on its
birthday
Hands out ready to embrace the comfort and secure feeling a
loved one has to offer
Knowing that someone will listen and understand what you
have always wanted to tell them
But could never get it out of your mouth.
The cloud starts to disappear, slowly
Like a cloudy day then the sun comes out.
And you can start to feel hope with the heat of the sun, as it
breaks through the cloud.
Your vision becomes so much clearer, life becomes much more
exciting.
You know you still tread carefully while fully embracing life's
wonders.
It's so good to TALK,
You eventually can turn your life around, by being proud of
yourself.
Talking, doing things that make you feel good, being proud of
how far you have come.
Knowing that there IS help out there.
You can see that light is coming closer and closer and getting
bigger and bigger.
And then finally there is light at end of the Tunnel.

Chapter Eleven

A few more years passed, and we had the good news that our fourth child was on the way. We had a lovely healthy wee girl – we called her Grace. This for me was now the perfect family.

It was a lovely feeling having a wonderful family and Gloria, my wife, who was so supportive of what I was doing. However, things didn't always go smoothly, and I had various spells of anxiety and still had flashbacks and nightmares. For years I used to get so angry in the weeks coming up to Christmas, about anything and nothing, and we just rode the storm – but it wasn't doing anybody any good. As the kids got older they began to watch out for my change of mood. Eventually Gloria suggested that we make an effort to include something tangible to remember all our lost loved ones at Christmas, including Ronnie and Gloria's sister Robena – who had died more recently – and her dad. Gloria suggested lighting candles for each of them, such a simple thing, but I find it gives me a focus as if they are with us, so we as a family light them on Christmas Day and Boxing Day and I find that very calming. Christmas became something to look forward to again.

My main aim was now to try and build the decorating business and carry on with my artwork. I wanted to develop my skills further and try to have more exhibitions professionally. The first one had gone very well so I was excited to try it again. I found this easy to do because my passion was with art and again it was all helping my mental health. I can honestly say that it never felt like work. I was so lucky being able to do something that I loved and when I would come home after a day's work I was not even stressed. I was in control, protecting my mental health.

I found that I needed to build myself an art studio because I needed the right surroundings to get the best out of what I do. And because I was working towards another exhibition, I needed the space to be able to display my work. The studio was amazing because I was able to sit at my drawing table and be in the zone. I would select the music I needed for that moment. All the things I needed were near me, I didn't need to get up when drawing and could get completely lost in each picture. I can only say from my own feelings that when I started to draw, the music on, me in the zone, it was like being on top of the world. This was something I feel that God put into me from birth. I had always felt that everyone has a talent and I think it would be a shame not to use it. I really feel that it was good to realise my talent early on in life, it was hard work but very stimulating developing it. I can say hand on heart that it saved my life.

That's why I knew that I had to try and get recognised as a professional pencil artist. As years went on I progressed. I continued to exhibit and sell my work and to date I have had nineteen exhibitions. Gloria has been on this journey with me since we met and she has always believed in me, giving me support and encouragement all the way through. This for me, having a mental health issue, is so important for my self-esteem.

Pencil drawing is a slow medium, but I found that when drawing I couldn't think about anything thing else. This was due to the concentration levels. Later on when I spoke to people doing the classes, they would say that too. The reason for this is because when you paint you can see the colours, your eyes are doing the work and you can think about other things but when drawing you are making a shade for a colour, so the concentration level rises so much that you can't think of other things. This is something that I and others have found.

When I am doing a drawing, I get so consumed in the picture, it is the most wonderful feeling; I am totally relaxed. Every time I do a picture, halfway through, I become so peaceful and just so, so glad to be alive. This may sound strange to people, but it happens to me every time.

I decided to venture out to bring my art into the community. This was going to be a big step but one I knew I had to take. My view was that there are not many pencil artists out there – also because it helped me mentally and was so stimulating, I felt that I had something unique. There was a great opportunity for people in general to do something that could help their mental health and wellbeing.

My first approach was to the education sector. I was lucky to get started in the primary school sector where teachers reported that after their art class, the children were in a better frame of mind for class and able to settle down to do their work. I then worked in the secondary and higher education sector. It was my goal to help people with stress, anxiety and mental health issues. I took time out wondering what way I could put a program together that works for everyone at any age. I did this and I started to make my contacts. My aim was to be an artist who provides art therapy. I was not a qualified art therapist because they do counselling alongside the art. I was very clear in what I was doing, just encouraging people to learn a new skill and to use the pencil drawing as a way to relax their minds.

I contacted different groups and organisations who needed help with their clients who suffered with various forms of mental illness. I advertised a basic drawing skills evening class and was amazed to have twenty people from all walks of life and ages. I was so excited to be able to do this and it was a great success. I also ran a class in the local college doing pencil drawing for relaxation.

I then turned my interest to getting daytime work. I worked in Derg Valley Day Care Centre, and I provided art therapy classes – I worked there for fifteen years. It was just lovely working with the elderly, they were enthusiastic and happy to be doing something new. I found some had different disabilities, but the program of art worked for all. I remember a wee lady of eighty-nine wanting to do the class. When I gave her the pencil to hold she said the last time she had ever done something like this was with a bit of chalk on a slate. Just amazing. They all found the classes very therapeutic and felt that the stress just left them. The POWER of pencil work. I remember a wee lady had such bad arthritis in her hands she was in so much pain. She said to me, 'I can't do the art.' I physically put the pencil into her hand, she started to shade and after about ten minutes I asked her how she was feeling. She said that she couldn't feel any pain but as soon as she put the pencil down the pain started again. It was the concentration on the drawing that helped her. For me it was such a positive experience and such a lovely feeling helping them to relax and forget about their troubles for a while. I found that helping them was helping me.

I also wanted to talk to different people who provide services for the vulnerable, people with disabilities, mental health issues and people in crisis. From talking to the professionals, I found that their view was the same as mine; it's all about helping people with their problems and mental health issues when they need it most. Not to let their situations get worse, protecting them and preventing them from getting to a point where there is no return and it's too late for help. Getting people, particularly men, to open up about their feelings can be hard, but offering them a relaxing situation such as a drawing class can help relax the mind and start that conversation. That's how I felt at the beginning, I was too scared to TALK and seek help, thinking that nobody cared. Also, there wasn't the amount of help available as there is today.

It's a lovely feeling waking up in the morning knowing that what you do makes a difference to people's lives.

I tried to get as much experience as I could in other areas of mental health, and with other agencies like alcoholism and drug addictions, post-traumatic stress and others. I got an opportunity to work with Solace, a group which provided support opportunities for people living with addiction in the community, so basically some of the clients came to class under the influence of drugs and alcohol. For me this was not a worry because I believed in my program and the power of pencil art being so stimulating.

My first day of class I had different age groups of men and women. I think I had about six or seven at the start, but word got around how much the clients enjoyed it that after a few weeks I was taking at least ten. For me it was such a privilege to be given this opportunity to work with the group, some of them were vulnerable adults. It was amazing what they achieved in the class, there were plenty of really good artists. They were able to show self-control, respect to me and others. It was a couple of hours that they could come, be calm and talk to each other. They all said that it was making a difference to them as individuals. The drawing had been able to break down many barriers within the class. There were many things said on how it helped each person, for me this was like gold dust.

From talking to my clients, I found that the drawing naturally brought out self-confidence, improved their concentration and motor skills, and relieved stress. It really gave each person a sense of achievement, helped to improve hand-eye coordination, and lastly it acts like a natural way of counselling through the art, for them to talk and build friendships. For me, I felt you can't put a price on helping people. We also had an opportunity to have an art exhibition. This was going to be an amazing achievement for the group. They were going to have to provide me with full commitment over so many weeks in order to create many drawings of their choice. The class was full of excitement and teamwork. The clients were so pleased with their work and a few of them couldn't believe what they had done. We finally got the exhibition together and it was held in the Arc Healthy Living Centre, Irvinestown. There were guests to come, funders and others. The event was a great success, I had a lot of budding artists walking around. I was so proud of being there and seeing what they had achieved, it was so special.

When life looks normal again.

Finally when I wake up in the morning and go outside
The sky so blue with the odd fluffy cloud drifting slowly, like
pieces of cotton wool.
The air so fresh, the breeze passing my face making my eyes
water as it passes.
The sounds of the birds talking to each other, yet in the dis-
tance I can hear
Machinery working in the fields, life is going on as normal.
Now my mind is so much clearer, I am able to think about
What I am going to do today
Nice thoughts, not negative ones, I know now I can embrace
anything that life throws at me
It's always a work in progress
But I know I have the tools to deal with my mental health and
to enjoy things and live my life to the full
Knowing that the shadow will always be hiding round the
corner
But life is for living, so good to be able to share it with other
people
And being able to help people when I can
I am so blessed to be able to face life head-on.

Masked Faces

Masks, Masks, Everywhere.

Walking down the street

You can see people walking and moving around quietly

Some say hello but they look strange with their masks on.

You can see fear in their eyes as they stare at you

And you can't tell who they are.

Like living in another world,

People talking to each other, all masked up but yet the body
language indicates caution, not to get too close when they
speak.

This hidden enemy lurking everywhere,

silently waiting to pounce on its next victim.

Not being able to see loved ones for so long,

It makes you feel you have no-one outside the defence of your
house,

Your sanctuary, the only place that feels safe.

The towns and villages seem like ghost towns,

buildings that were always busy,

full of excitement and banter, now lying like ghost ships in a
harbour.

Even in the countryside, how quiet the roads are,

less cars and lorries, but full of music from the birdsong

The country roads are full of people walking to clear their
minds

From the stresses of this grip of fear that cocoons us all.

But we know that the scientists will prevail

We all pull together and with love and harmony we will get
our world back

The way it used to be.

Chapter Twelve

My name, and what I did, was obviously being talked about by different groups. I got an opportunity to work with Families Moving On based in Omagh. Some of my clients had been impacted by the Omagh bomb so I was working with clients who had post-traumatic stress and anxiety. When I started, the class was small, but it increased after a few weeks and I ended up with about twelve clients. They were a lovely group, they embraced my program. There were different age groups, friendships were made, and the banter was good. The class not only helped people with their traumas, but helped with the social skills of talking and enjoying each other's company. For me this was just the icing on the cake for what I do. We were able to build confidence in their artwork, many worked on different pictures. A lot of the group said that the classes were making a difference to them mentally and they all found it very stimulating. We even got a chance for them to design and draw their own Christmas cards.

There was an opportunity for the class to do drawings on peace and reconciliation. After the pictures were completed, there was an event to present framed pictures to schools in the Omagh area – a cross community event. I am so privileged and honoured to have been a part of this group and having them put so much skill and feeling into what they achieved. I have been with this group for about four years now and it will continue again when COVID restrictions are lifted. For me being an artist and doing drawing for therapy art, it's amazing being able to use my experience and skill to help clients achieve beautiful art pieces. Also by doing the art, they were able to feel good about themselves and help their mental health with the stimulation that pencil art provides. I am so lucky to be able to do this in my community and try to help in this fight against mental health issues.

Keeping in this area I worked with several groups whose clients were dealing with PTSD, depression and anxiety, some of whom had been affected by 'The Troubles'. This was so rewarding for me because I was still doing something that was good for me while I was helping people at the same time.

My work took me to Inspire Wellbeing in Omagh, this was an opportunity to work and provide art therapy to a mainly younger group of clients. The group that I worked with were amazing. They took to the program that I was using. They all found that the art really helped them to chill out and they looked forward to it every week. It really helped them to work as a group, breaking down any barriers they might have on meeting people. One thing that I observed was that they all were very proud of their artwork and they all communicated with each other, they all had great confidence in the class. They became really good artists and they produced amazing work, some even started to do their own work at home and would bring extra pieces into the class to show them off. This was a great success for me to see them develop the skill and get so much out of it. I also worked with Prospects in Castlederg, they were a group supporting Mental Wellbeing, they provided the same service as Inspire. This was an older group, and they loved the art also.

I also worked with an ADHD group in Enniskillen, it was lovely to see the way the art calmed some of the group, it showed me that the art therapy worked well with people of different needs. For me I was living the dream of helping people of all walks of life, helping them to de-stress, and some of my clients just wanted to draw for the fun of it.

I was doing work for Fermanagh and Omagh District Council. There was an opportunity to work with a cancer group and the class was held in Enniskillen Castle. The first morning of the class I didn't know how many people there would be, and it was the first time I'd worked with a cancer group. They were going through treatment or in remission. The class had about twelve in it, all women. What a good class, we had a lot of banter and laughs. The women took to the drawing so quickly and they produced some lovely work. They too found the drawing really helped them to relax and they said that when doing it they couldn't think about anything else. When I listened to some of their stories it was so nice that I was part of their healing process, mentally and emotionally.

As I continued to do this work in the community I was invited to talk to a group in the Strule Arts Centre, Omagh. The event was the International Day for Persons with Disabilities. I was keen to do the talk because I felt I had a story to tell that could be of benefit to more people and I think if my story could help just one person then it would be worthwhile.

I was going there representing the council as an art

therapy tutor and my topic was Creativity – A Link to Improve Wellbeing. I really didn't know what to expect. I thought it was an informal chat to ten or twelve people but boy, was I wrong! I was met by the organisers and shown into the auditorium. It looked huge and there were at least 100 people in the hall. The council chairman welcomed me and said, 'Trevor, you are the third speaker. Come with me, I will bring you to your seat,' it was at the front of the stage. I was like a rabbit caught in the headlights of a car; I didn't know what to think. I sat down and thought this was going to be one of the biggest tests for my own mental health. I had never done anything on this scale before and how was I going to cope?

The chairman got up to start proceedings and he was speaking into a microphone for all to hear. The first speaker was a man talking about the help that's available for people with disabilities. The second speaker was a friendly woman from Health and Social Wellbeing, she gave a PowerPoint presentation and her talk came across so professionally with facts and figures, and then there was me! I had no notes and my brain was going ten to the dozen. I was nervous but in a good way and all I could think of was how am I going to follow that?

Then this wee voice came into my head saying, 'You want to talk about your story and life experiences, there's no better opportunity than this.' With all the relevant agencies in the room from all over I was getting the chance to talk about the experiences I had had with my own mental health and how, through my own use of art as a healing tool, I could connect to what I was doing in the classes.

I was called to the stage and for a few seconds things just stopped, but I had to make a move.

I remember not looking at anyone but just spotting the podium and microphone and quietly walking up to them. I pulled the mic down to my level and took a deep breath.

I suddenly had the confidence, and as if there were only ten people in the room, I started to tell my story from the beginning to the present day, working with groups with art therapy. As I was talking I looked around the room, I did notice a few people agreeing with me and nodding their heads on some matters. I just told my story from the heart and everyone in the room had their eyes fixed on me, listening – apart from my own voice, there was silence. When I came to the end of my talk I thanked everyone for giving me the opportunity. As soon as I was finished the room erupted with applause, people were even standing up for me. Boy I was so taken aback from the reaction. I left the podium and went down to my seat beside the second speaker. She turned to me and said, 'Fantastic, Trevor. You just stood up there with no notes, told your story about your mental health, and there was me with my PowerPoints!' She said, 'You spoke from the heart, we all could feel the emotion in your story.' There was a half-time break for coffee but people were still coming over to me to congratulate me on such a moving story, they said they wished more men could come out and talk like that.

I didn't do the talk to get praise, this was just my story locked away for years wanting to get out and be used to help other people with a mental health condition. The reaction was more than I could have expected, but for me this was the starting point to be able to relate my story, and if it can help one other person then it is worth it.

I just felt I was representing other men who have mental

health issues – really a voice for all of us. I do feel that men have this macho thing where they may feel that it's a weakness to talk about how they feel. Take it from me, it is not. I praise anyone who has the courage to open their hearts and ask for help. It is good to TALK.

I came home buzzing from that event and feeling free because I had never spoken to a big crowd of people like that before. I knew now that this was something else that I can provide to help with mental health. I then got an opportunity to have a talk with a Walking Football group at Ballinamallard Football Club. I was so pleased to get this chance to speak to a men's club in my own area. When I got there we had a cup of tea and there was some general chat among the men. My first talk in Omagh was to professional people working in mental health and disability services but this next one was the first time to really speak to a group of ordinary guys and I knew most of them.

I was introduced to the group and I started to tell them my story. The guys were great listeners which made things easier for me. I talked for a good forty-five minutes and when I finished the group applauded me. I invited them to ask me any questions and a few could relate to different aspects of my talk. Some of the guys said that it took a lot of courage to talk so openly about the problems I had had but I said I did it in the hope that it would encourage other men to talk if they needed to. If it planted a seed to help someone else then that is a good thing. One man came to me discreetly to ask about some of my symptoms, he could relate this to someone he knew and thanked me for helping him to realise that the symptoms he was seeing in his friend were something that he should be aware of in order to help. Being able to get that response was amazing, we all need to talk about our problems sometimes.

I remember seeing an ad on TV, it was from BT and they said it was good to talk, but for me I could use this in my own story because it was so true – talk to people, share your thoughts, it can really take the pressure off.

I went home after the group talk with a buzz, feeling that it's all about helping people if they suffer from stress, anxiety, depression or other mental health issues.

The Sun Flower - Symbol of Light and Hope

The Sunflower stands so upright,
Like a telescope being able to see all over the country side.
Shining like the sun, with its beautiful bright yellow colour.
A happy colour, one that cheers you up quickly when you see it
Its stem so long shows strength and pride as it towers over the
ground
A symbol of light and hope
For all who suffer from mental illness
Symbolising that we all can be successfully treated
Stand tall, be happy and embrace life, with the sun on our face.

Chapter Thirteen

Working with different groups and organisations has been a fantastic experience for me and one that is developing day by day. There are so many people who need a helping hand for them to complete their life journey. Everyone I work with at art therapy has their own reasons for being there, the important thing for me is that by working with the calming and therapeutic effect of pencil art I can make life a little bit easier for them. My experiences of working with all ages is that all who took part in classes found that it made them feel much better. Some clients went on to do their own art because they progressed so much. I have been so lucky in my life to come from what happened to me, to be able to turn my passion into a skill that has helped people make a change and improve their way of thinking. It has helped my mental health also, but in my opinion, mental wellness is always a work in progress, learning ways to cope and living your best life.

In the past few years, alongside the classes, I have had the confidence to talk to people about my own mental health. This has led to people hearing my story and seeming to feel comfortable enough with me to open up about their own mental health issues. For me this has been a humbling experience, that people can trust me enough because they know that I have felt many of the same things.

The reasons for writing this book were to show people that there is nothing to be ashamed of when they need to talk about their issues with mental health, and not to be afraid to talk about anything that is worrying them, no matter what. Men in particular have this stigma about asking for help. They probably think that it's a sign of weakness, not very macho. Well to all you guys out there, being able to talk can save your life. Being able to share your worries can take a weight off your shoulders and can make life so much easier to deal with.

So all you men out there, it's good to TALK, TALK, TALK.

I was told when I got help that it was important to get the balance right. Art was my relaxation, it allowed me to be occupied at something I enjoyed without worrying about anything else. Sport was my next thing that allowed me to have fun and exercise and because I played tennis outside, I got plenty of fresh air. Also most importantly I got my aggression out. This helped my feelings. Then I had my home life, doing all the little things and spending time with my lovely family.

I feel that it's important to spend time with family and loved ones but even though it might sound selfish, it's also important to take yourself away from family and have time for yourself. Doing something that only you enjoy is so important, whether you walk, pursue a hobby, or something just for you to chill out with.

I have found over the years that having these practices in place has helped my general wellbeing, it's a form of discipline, making it a part of life is key to me having the tools to protect my mental health. Also I feel I have developed a resilience to help me going forward.

We as a family, like any other, have gone through some challenges while bringing up our children. Guiding them through childhood and teenage years, working towards their goals at school and further education, achieving what they want to do as adults, we always were there to give encouragement, love and hugs, in happy times, and sad. It was teamwork, but I couldn't have asked for a better person than Gloria to share this journey in our life. The kids are adults now finding their own way, but they know that we are here day and night for them if they need us. I always remind them that it's good to talk, we are always here to share and help.

In the last few years I lost my mum and dad, but I found that the resilience I have built up helped me when they passed away. I am so grateful for the opportunity of life that they give me as a child and into adulthood. I am from a big family and I'm sure they found it tough at times bringing us up, but they were rock-solid on love, kindness and support.

Chapter Fourteen

The past few years have been extraordinary to say the least. We could never have imagined that the whole world would be affected by COVID-19. When you see this silent killer affecting so many people, and seeing so many deaths, you wonder how are we meant to get through it? However, the development of the vaccine in such a short space of time has given us hope. I feel that because of the fear of the disease and the lockdowns it has been so hard on people's mental health, and it has made us look at life differently. Jobs are important but there is no price you can put on life. We are going to have to live with COVID, just like the flu, there will always be cases and deaths but we have to try and live our lives with some normality. It might never be the same, but we will all have to adjust to the new 'normal'.

I do feel that mental health problems will be massive, even some people having to work from home for so long will find it hard to integrate again. So many things that we do to enjoy life have been affected. Long COVID will be a huge problem for people who will need continued help. I feel that I have coped better with the threat due to the resilience I developed because of my own mental health over my lifetime. It definitely helped me deal with this pandemic mentally. Now that the vaccination program is here due to the hard work of the scientists, we have some protection to move on through this dark time. We will need all available help that can be given for mental health. A lot of people will need help for years.

When I look at myself over the years dealing with mental health, I have come to realise that I will never be totally free from my problems, but I have learned to live with it and make a good life for myself by doing the things that make me happy and being surrounded by positive people.

I am so blessed to be given that second chance of life and finding peace in myself. I have also found my role in life – using my gift of art and transforming it into something that can help other people and I know doing art therapy now for sixteen years with so many groups, I have made a difference. You can't put a price on that feeling. I have been so lucky doing something that I love. Also, I have been pleased meeting so many wonderful people, and having so many good, supportive friends. It means a lot to have a good network of people around you. The number one supportive network I have had in my life is my wife Gloria and our lovely family, Ross, Peter, Daniel and Grace, they have always been there for me in good times and bad times.

I sometimes feel that a mental health problem is like dropping a stone into a calm pond. When it hits the surface huge ripples emerge out from the centre, and as time goes on, they get smaller and smaller until its calm again, but the water is still there. So it is with mental wellness, you start with this turmoil and as time goes on and you are getting help – talking to people, doing things that are good for you – life gets better and you become calmer, able to cope and live a life that you are happy with, but you always have to remember that the scars are still there.

I have always wanted to tell this story because I have carried it in my head for such a long time. COVID has given me the time to get down to it. Being able to talk about it and sharing it with other people has helped me mentally. Also, I hope that it can help other people to open up and share a problem, don't let it fester and make life even harder. It has been, and still is, a fantastic feeling knowing that I can make a difference.

Finally, these words have meant so much to me: IT'S GOOD TO TALK.

About the Author

Trevor Verner is an artist and art therapy tutor who lives with his wife and family in Ballinamallard, Co Fermanagh.

Trevor has been a professional artist for thirty-five years, his medium is pencil.

He has had nineteen exhibitions – some solo and some with other artists.

This is a memoir of Trevor's journey with mental illness and recovery and his efforts to bring his art out into the community to help other people.

Trevor says, 'Working so much with my art and knowing the benefits it has for mental health, I decided fifteen years ago to take a program out into the community. I was lucky to get the opportunity to work with all different types of groups and using my program to change lives in mental health. I have now worked in many areas of mental health and I hope to continue to help people.'

Acknowledgements

Thank you to my lovely wife, Gloria, whose patience and support have kept me going, I wouldn't be where I am today without her.

Thanks also to our kids – to Ross for all the technical help, to Peter, Daniel and Grace for their encouragement, to Anna for my Facebook page and to Lesa who has brought our beautiful granddaughters into the world.

To bestselling author, my manager at Inspire Mental Health, Omagh, Co Tyrone, Emma Weaver, thank you for your kind support over the past year and being a great mentor for me to achieve this book. You have always been there for guidance, thank you.

Thanks to Dr Tim Bingham MRCGP for his contribution to this book, and to Mullan Pharmacy, Enniskillen, Co Fermanagh for their generous sponsorship.

Thank you, Karen McDermott, of KMD books, for this wonderful opportunity to get my story out there for mental health.

All proceeds from the sale of the book will be going back into mental health services in Fermanagh and Tyrone.

I would like to thank Mullan Boutique Pharmacy for
their kind sponsorship towards the book.